EUROPEAN DESIGNS

HART PICTURE
ARCHIVES

European
Designs

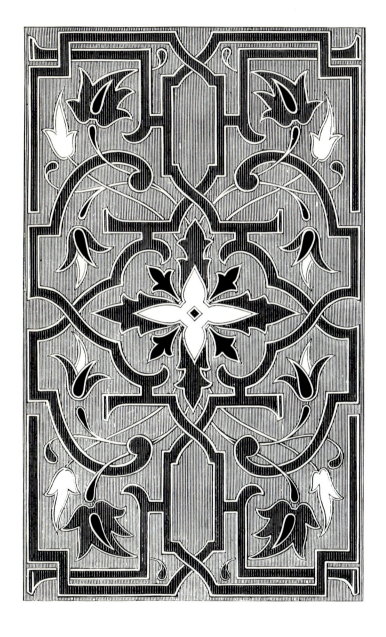

Compiled by Robert Sietsema

Hart Publishing Company, Inc. ● New York City

ISBN NO. 08055-1268-3 (PAPERBACK 08055-0331-5)

MANUFACTURED IN THE UNITED STATES OF AMERICA

CONTENTS

HOW TO USE THIS BOOK

EUROPEAN DESIGNS is a collection of over 400 pictures of many periods culled from 14 known sources. These pictures have been divided into 5 categories.

All these pictures are in the public domain, and may be used for any purpose without fee or permission. Most of the pictures derive from books and magazines for which copyright is not in force. Others are copyrighted by Hart Publishing Company, but are now released to the public for general use.

So as not to clutter a caption, the source is given an abbreviated designation. Full publication data may be found in the *Sources* section, in which all sources are listed in alphabetical order, with the full title of the book or magazine, the publisher, and the date of publication. The *Sources* section commences on page 127.

Two of the pictures are halftones, and are designated by a square symbol at the end of each caption. These pictures, too, are suitable for reproduction, but the user is alerted to rescreen such a picture or convert it into line. All other pictures can be reproduced directly in line.

British Designs

Inlaid ornament. *Gewerbehalle, Vol. 6*

Tablecloth design by C. Berger, late 19th century. *Gewerbehalle, Vol. 2*

Porcelain design. *Gewerbehalle, Vol. 7*

Carved wood ornament, 15th century. *Encyclopedia of Ornament*

British Designs continued

Woodcut by Gertrude Hermes. *Studio*

Ribbon. *Industry of Nations*

Silk design. *Industry of Nations*

Heraldic lion, 13th century. *Pattern Design*

British Designs continued

Book cover design in the Art Nouveau style. *Studio* □

Art Nouveau book ornament. *Studio*

British Designs continued

Irish drapery design. *Gewerbehalle, Vol. 12*

Painted ornament for a railway carriage. *Workshop, Vol. 2*

British Designs continued

Ante-pendiums, early 16th century. *Encyclopedia of Ornament*

Border of lace veil. *Industry of Nations*

Embroidered waistcoat.
Industry of Nations

Irish damask napkin. *Industry of Nations*

Victorian Stencils

British Designs continued

Material for a cashmere dress, made in Scotland. *Industry of Nations*

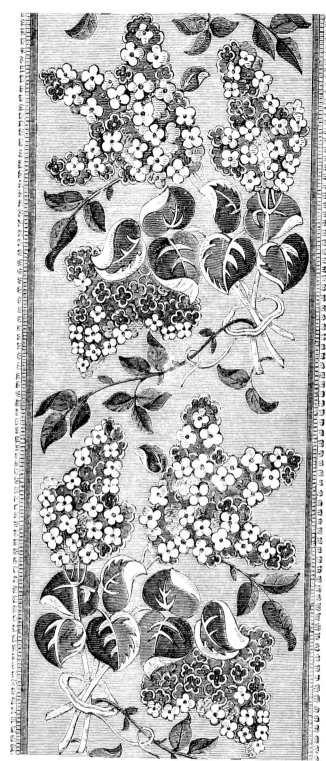

Ribbon. *Industry of Nations*

Victorian Stencils

Celtic interlaced ornament. *Outlines*

Gold brocade pattern. *Industry of Nations*

British Designs continued

Arms of Great Britain and Ireland. *English Encyclopedia*

Embroidery on a pair of men's drawers.
Industry of Nations

Victorian Stencils

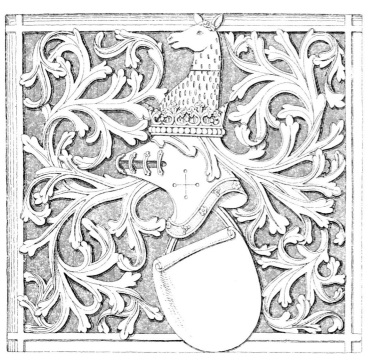
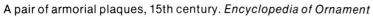

A pair of armorial plaques, 15th century. *Encyclopedia of Ornament*

Art Nouveau book ornament. *Studio*

British Designs continued

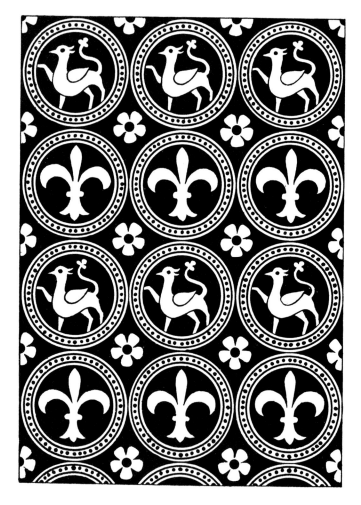

Medieval diaper ornament, four examples. *Outlines*

Embroidered cloth. *Industry of Nations*

Table cloth, one corner. *Industry of Nations*

British Designs continued

Carpet design by F.T. Parris. *Industry of Nations*

Brocaded silk by Lewis & Allenby, of London. *Industry of Nations*

Embroidery trimming. *Industry of Nations*

Stained glass window, York Cathedral. *Encyclopedia of Ornament*

British Designs continued

Archbishop's cape. *Industry of Nations*

Three stencil designs. *Victorian Stencils*

British Designs continued

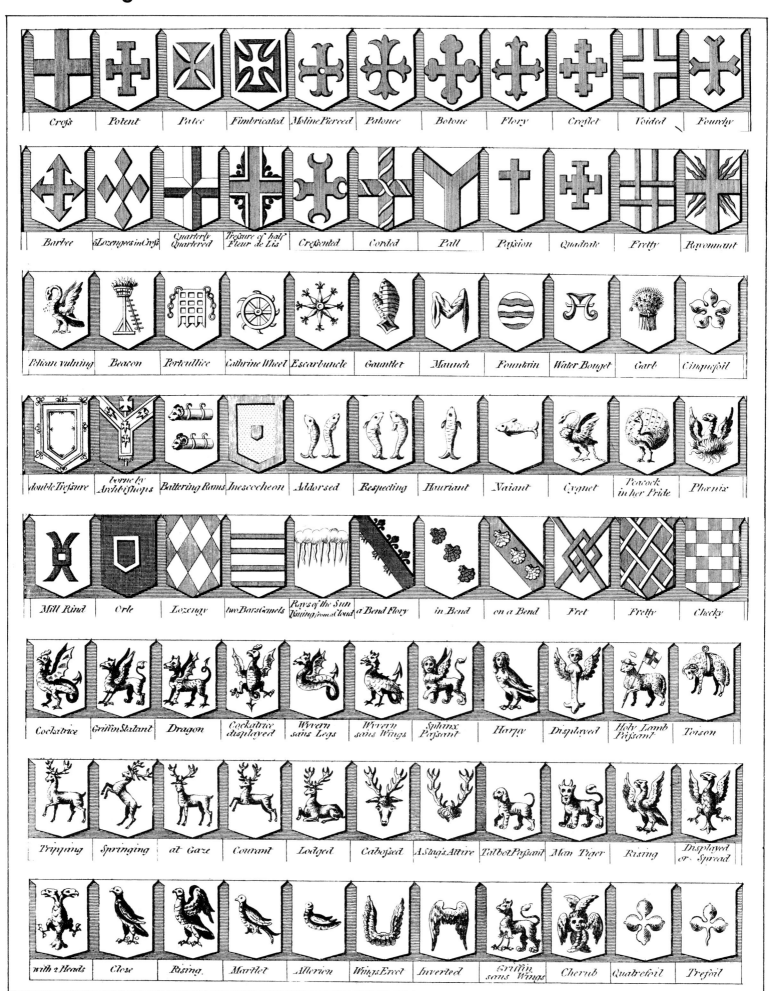

Cross	Potent	Patee	Fimbricated	Moline Pierced	Patonce	Botone	Flory	Crestet	Voided	Fourchy
Barbee	6 Lozenges in Cross	Quarterly Quartered	Tressure of half Fleur de Lis	Crescented	Corded	Pall	Passion	Quadrate	Fretty	Rayonnant
Pelican vulning	Beacon	Portcullice	Cathrine Wheel	Escarbuncle	Gauntlet	Maunch	Fountain	Water Bouget	Garb	Cinquefoil
double Tressure	borne by Archbishops	Battering Rams	Inescocheon	Addorsed	Respecting	Hauriant	Naiant	Cygnet	Peacock in her Pride	Phœnix
Mill Rind	Orle	Lozengy	two Bars Gemels	Rays of the Sun Issuing from a cloud	a Bend Flory	in Bend	on a Bend	Fret	Fretty	Checky
Cockatrice	Griffin Statant	Dragon	Cockatrice displayed	Wyvern sans Legs	Wyvern sans Wings	Sphinx Passant	Harpy	Displayed	Holy Lamb Passant	Toison
Tripping	Springing	at Gaze	Courant	Lodged	Cabossed	A Stag's Attire	Talbot Passant	Man Tiger	Rising	Displayed or Spread
with 2 Heads	Close	Rising	Martlet	Allerion	Wings Erect	Inverted	Griffin sans Wings	Cherub	Quatrefoil	Trefoil

Heraldic charges. *English Encyclopedia*

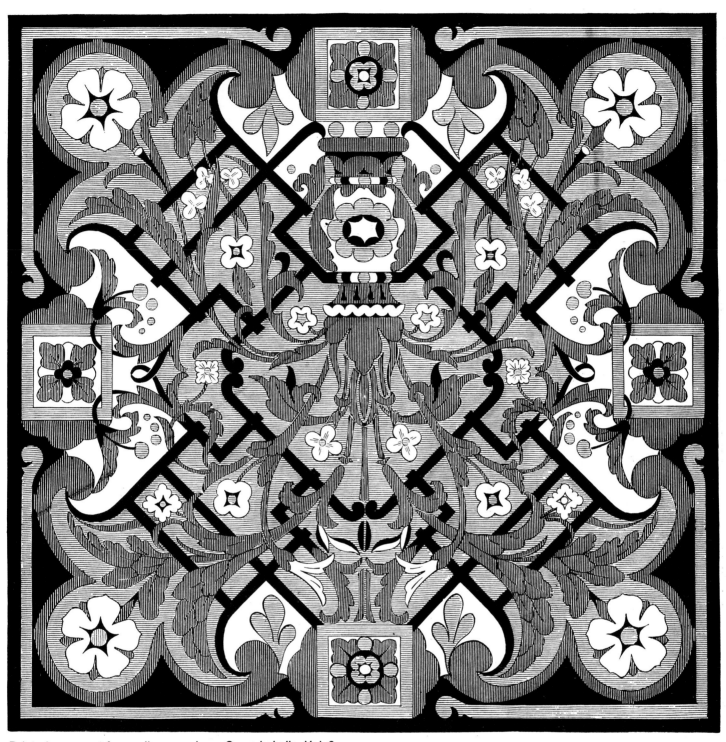

Painted ornament for a railway carriage. *Gewerbehalle, Vol. 6*

Carved ornament on a box, late 15th century. *Encyclopedia of Ornament*

British Designs continued

Four stained glass window designs based on oak and maple leaf motifs, Canterbury Cathedral. *Encyclopedia of Ornament*

Scottish cradle cover. *Industry of Nations*

British Designs continued

Silk pattern. *Industry of Nations*

Furniture damask. *Industry of Nations*

Poplin pattern. *Industry of Nations*

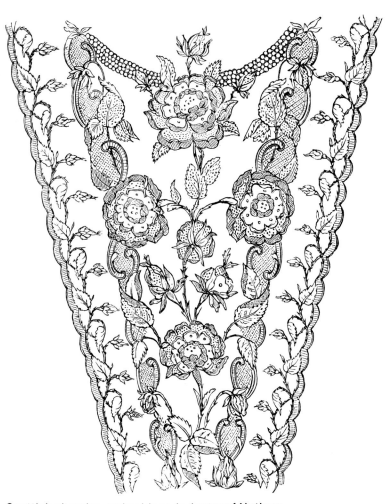

Scottish chemise embroidery. *Industry of Nations*

Ribbon. *Industry of Nations*

Carpet design. *Industry of Nations*

Motif for wool design. *Industry of Nations*

Victorian Stencils

British Designs continued

Art Nouveau motifs. *Type & Design*

Art Nouveau design, positive and negative. *Studio*

Vignettes from velvet hangings, late 6th century.
Encyclopedia of Ornament.

Sixteenth century lace pattern. *Encyclopedia of Ornament*

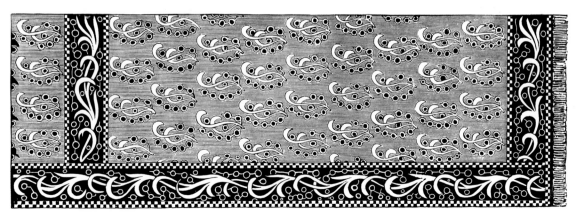

Cashmere scarf, made in Scotland. *Industry of Nations*

French Designs

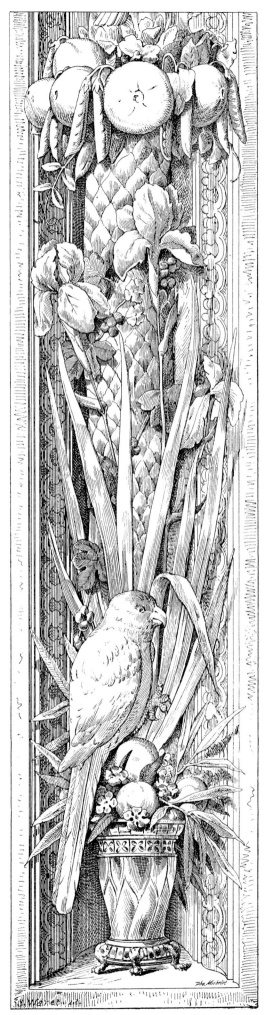

Tapestry border, 17th century. *L'Art, Vol. 20*

Hand-painted plate by the Cazin brothers, early 20th century. *L'Art, Vol. 37*

Composition by M. Emile Cause, 19th century. *L'Art, Vol. 31*

French Designs continued

Tragic masks, Paris Opera House. *Gewerbehalle, Vol. 9*

Mosaic in the cathedral of Monreale, 12th century. *Gewerbehalle, Vol. 10*

Paneling for a vestibule, 19th century. *Gewerbehalle, Vol. 10*

French Designs continued

Two geometrical designs. *L'Art, Vol. 14*

Vignettes from a pavement. *L'Art, Vol. 12*

Composition with mice, by M.D. Alliot of the National School of Design. *L'Art, Vol. 35*

Ceramic border. *L'Art, Vol. 27*

Conventional foliage. *Outlines*

French Designs continued

Textile pattern, 19th century. *L'Art Vol. 16*

Border design. *Outlines*

Tapestry ornament. *L'Art, Vol. 26*

Conventional foliage, from tapestries. *Outlines*

A pair of stained glass windows from the Church of *Saint Jean aux Bois*, near Compiegne, dating from the 13th century. *L'Art, Vol. 7*

French Designs continued

Various radial designs. *Gewerbehalle, Vol. 11*

A pair of floral motifs by Elisabeth Voysard. *L'Art, Vol. 5*

Gothic relief, Notre Dame Cathedral. *Gewerbehalle, Vol. 3*

French Designs continued

Faience for a bathroom, 19th century. *Gewerbehalle, Vol. 10*

Border designed by M. Clerget in the Moresque style, 19th century. *Workshop, Vol. 9*

Tapestry. *Gewerbehalle, Vol. 8*

French Designs continued

Conventional foliage. *Outlines*

Silver and enamel box shown at the Vienna World's Fair. *Gewerbehalle, Vol. 12*

Bookcover by Petit & Massard of Paris. *Workshop, Vol. 4*

French Designs continued

Book cover, 16th century. *L'Art, Vol. 8*

Book cover bearing the Montmorency coat of arms, 16th century. *L'Art, Vol. 5*

French Designs continued

Enamel basin, 13th century. *L'Art, Vol. 18*

Flemish funeral slab, 15th century. *L'Art, Vol. 22*

French Designs continued

Facing ornamented manuscript pages, 17th century. *L'Art, Vol. 21*

French Designs continued

A pair of "twines", or interlaced designs. *L'Art, Vol. 5*

Textile pattern, 19th century. *L'Art, Vol. 16*

Painted tissue, 18th century. *L'Art, Vol. 4*

French Designs continued

Eighteenth century lace. *L'Art, Vol. 12*

French Designs continued

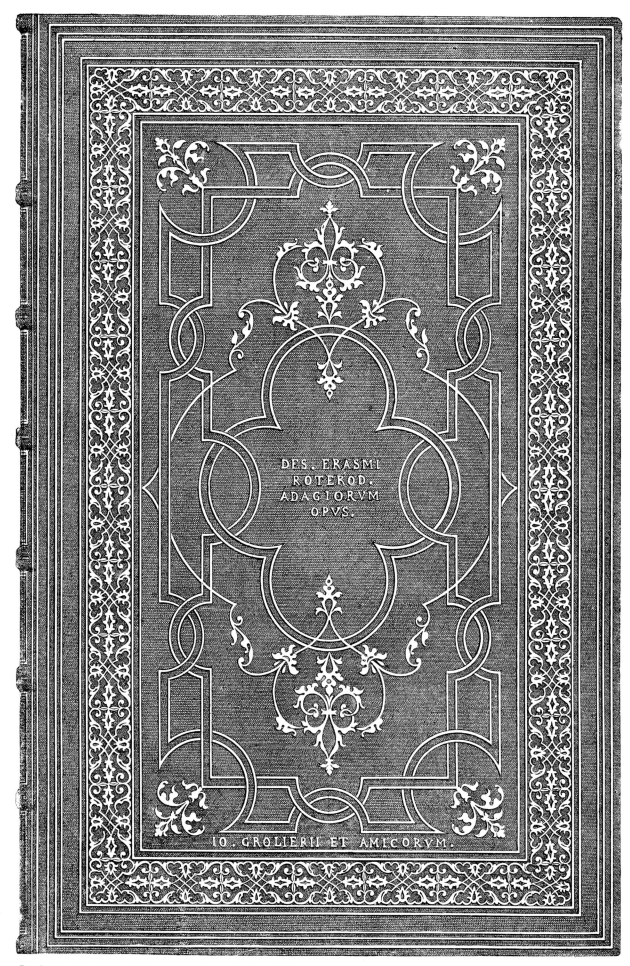

Book cover, tooled gold on green sheep-leather, 16th century. *L'Art, Vol. 22*

Coffer in tooled leather, with unicorn and stag, 15th century. *L'Art, Vol. 21*

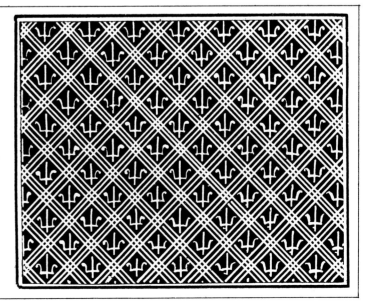

Manuscript ornament, 14th century. *Pattern Design*

French Designs continued

Flemish printed tissue, 14th century. *L'Art, Vol. 22*

Ornate Archbishop's crozier, 12th century, with detail. *L'Art, Vol. 24*

French Designs continued

Four compositions by M. Leon Rudnicki of the National School of Decorative Arts, late 19th century. *L'Art, Vol. 33*

Finest quality Lyon embroidered silk, 18th century. *L'Art, Vol. 12*

French Designs continued

Flemish wallpaper design, 18th century. *L'Art, Vol. 47*

Norman chimera, 14th century. *L'Art, Vol. 16*

Norman pilaster, 12th century. *Encyclopedia of Ornament*

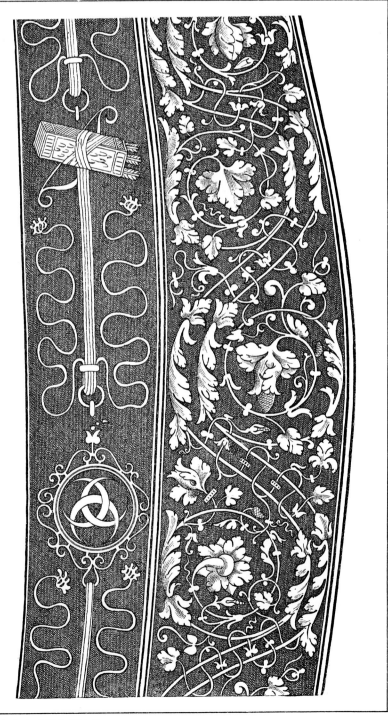

Ornamentation on the legs of a suit of armor, damascened in gold, 16th century. *L'Art, Vol. 9*

French Designs continued

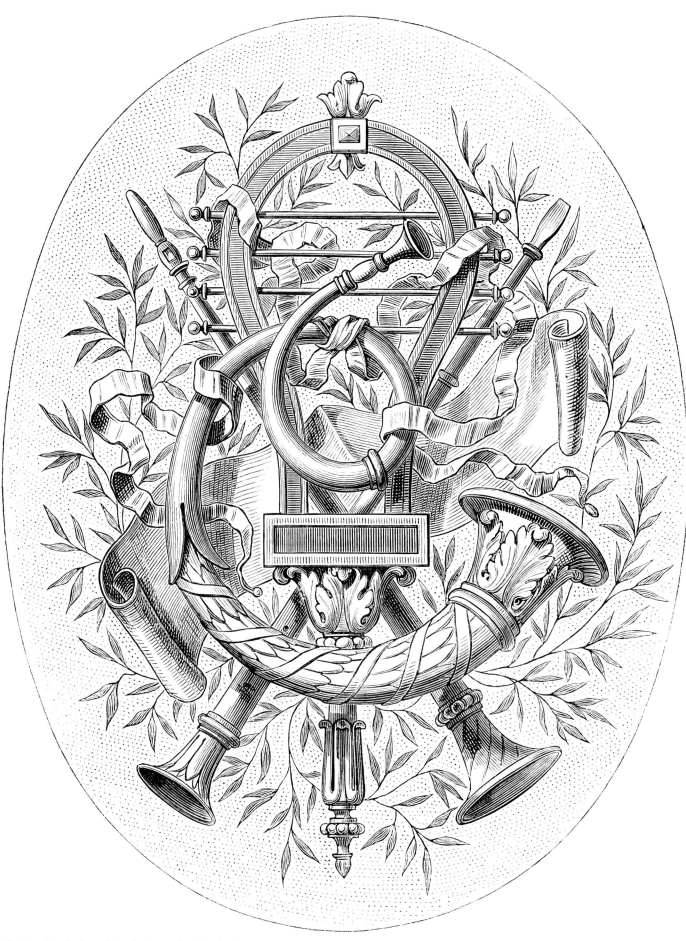

Cartouche designed by A. Denvelle. *Workshop, Vol. 6*

Modern diaper. *Outlines*

German Designs

Pattern for church vestments, white silk damask with gold. *Workshop, Vol. 2*

Vase ornament, late 19th century. *Gewerbehalle, Vol. 10*

Medieval German diaper. *Outlines*

German Designs continued

Berlin tapestry in the Moresque style, early 19th century. *Gewerbehalle, Vol. 6*

Medieval fabric design. *Gewerbehalle, Vol. 2*

Austrian border design by Friedrich Fischbach. *Gewerbehalle, Vol. 3*

German Designs continued

Porcelain ornament, 19th century. *Gewerbehalle, Vol. 1*

Modern geometric designs. *Gewerbehalle, Vol. 2*

Ceiling design from a villa in Stuttgart. *Gewerbehalle, Vol. 10*

German Designs continued

Album cover exhibited at the Vienna World's Fair. *Gewerbehalle, Vol. 8*

A pair of designs by Professor Herdtle of Stuttgart. *Gewerbehalle, Vol. 2*

Diaper from a painting by Burkmaier, late 15th century. *Workshop, Vol. 2*

German Designs continued

Tapestry design. *Gewerbehalle, Vol. 5*

St. Stephen's dalmatic, 13th century, with detail. *L'Art, Vol. 24*

German Designs continued

Fabric design. *Gewerbehalle, Vol. 11*

Tablecloth in linen damask. *Gewerbehalle, Vol. 6*

German Designs continued

Stained-glass windows, 19th century. *Gewerbehalle, Vol. 7*

Ceramic ornament. *Gewerbehalle, Vol. 4*

Gothic altar cloth. *Gewerbehalle, Vol. 6*

German Designs continued

Hand-painted plate. *Workshop, Vol. 8*

Embroidered valance, gold on red, 16th century. *Gewerbehalle, Vol. 8*

Gothic stonework.
Encyclopedia of Ornament

Vignette by Professor F. Fischbach of Hanau. *Workshop, Vol. 13*

Floor design, in marble, 16th century. *Gewerbehalle, Vol. 2*

German Designs continued

Border on a wall. *Gewerbehalle, Vol. 2*

Motif from a tablecloth, late 19th century. *Gewerbehalle, Vol. 11*

Medieval diaper. *Outlines*

German Designs continued

Medieval Dutch diaper. *Outlines*

Woven fabric, 15th century. *Gewerbehalle, Vol. 6*

German Designs continued

Design for isinglass, late 19th century. (Isinglass is made from the bladders of Russian sturgeons.) *Gewerbehalle, Vol. 2*

Stained glass windows, Bensheim Cathedral. *Gewerbehalle, Vol. 5*

German Designs continued

Painting dated 1472. *Encyclopedia of Ornament*

Border of a vase. *Gewerbehalle, Vol. 6*

Furniture ornament. *Gewerbehalle, Vol. 9*

German Designs continued

Shield depicting the four seasons, 17th century. *Weapons & Armor*

Embroidery design, 19th century. *Gewerbehalle, Vol. 9*

German Designs continued

Ornament on a vase. *Gewerbehalle, Vol. 5*

Tapestry design, 19th century. *Gewerbehalle, Vol. 11*

Architectural ornament. *Gewerbehalle, Vol. 3*

Design from a planter for flowers. *Gewerbehalle, Vol. 9*

Viennese painted ceiling. *Gewerbehalle, Vol. 7*

Italian Designs

Floor mosaic, Palermo Cathedral. *Gewerbehalle, Vol. 6*

Wainscoting in the sacristy of Santa Maria Cathedral, Verona. *Workshop, Vol. 2*

Linen design, 19th century. *Gewerbehalle, Vol. 3*

Italian Designs continued

Fabric design. *Gewerbehalle, Vol. 10*

Frame designed by Rinaldo Barbetti, 19th century. *Workshop, Vol. 6*

Italian Designs continued

Venetian embroidery, 17th century. *L'Art, Vol. 35*

Mosaic from Monreale Cathedral near Palermo, 12th century. *Workshop, Vol. 6*

Design for intarsia in Santa Maria Cathedral of Organo, 15th century. *Gewerbehalle, Vol. 12*

Italian Designs continued

Dish, 16th century, shown actual size. *L'Art, Vol. 24*

Late Gothic design, taken from a painting by Ambrogio Fossano, dated 1490. *Gewerbehalle, Vol. 2*

Ceramic border design. *Workshop, Vol. 7*

Italian Designs continued

Door in the Palazzo Vecchio in Florence. *Workshop, Vol. 8*

Helmet with black ground damascened in gold, 16th century.
Weapons & Armor

Italian Designs continued

Mosaic from Pavia, 18th century. *Workshop, Vol. 8*

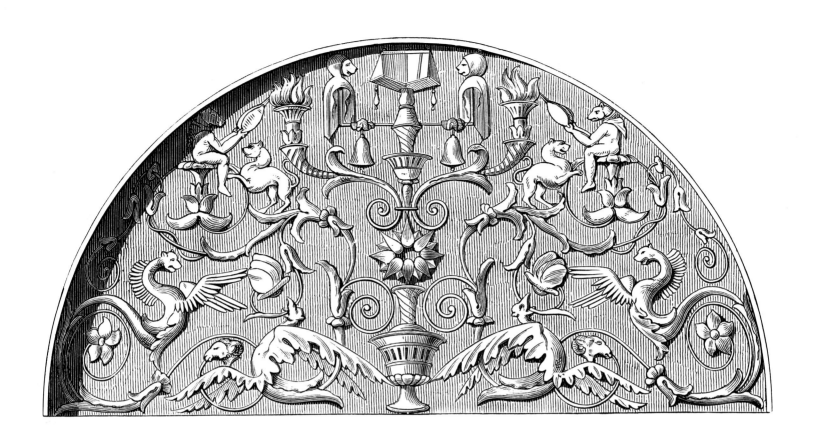

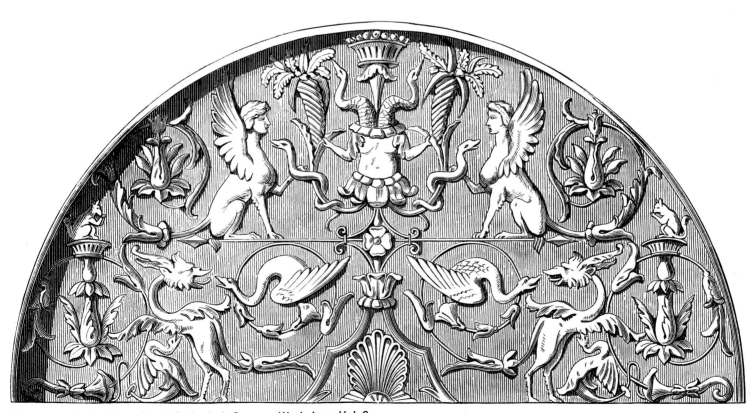

Ornaments in the Santa Maria Cathedral, Organo. *Workshop, Vol. 6*

Italian Designs continued

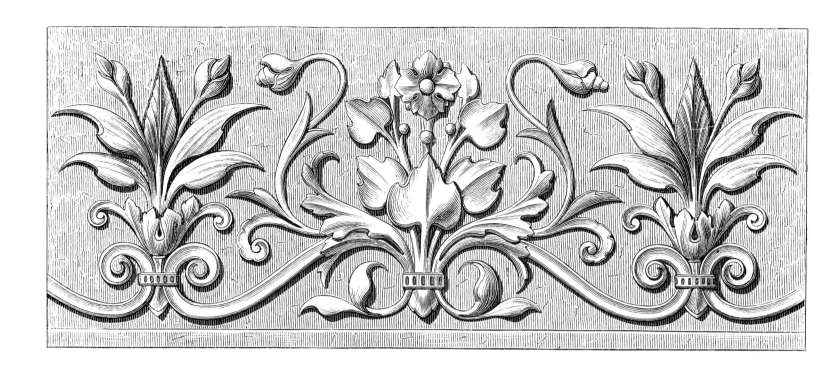

Renaissance ornament, two examples. *Gewerbehalle, Vol. 5*

Gothic fabric showing Saracenic influence, late 12th century. *Period Furnishings*

Italian Designs continued

Fragment of a painted ceiling, 16th century. *L'Art, Vol. 22*

Interlaced design by Leonardo da Vinci. *Pattern Design*

Textile ornaments, 15th century. *Pattern Design*

Italian Designs continued

Medieval Sicilian diaper. *Outlines*

Silk design with angels swinging censers, 14th century. *L'Art, Vol. 25* ☐

Border design. *Gewerbehalle, Vol. 6*

Italian Designs continued

Hand-painted Sicilian dish, 15th century. *L'Art, Vol. 16*

Ivory inlay on a piece of furniture, 16th century. *L'Art, Vol. 28*

Miscellaneous Designs

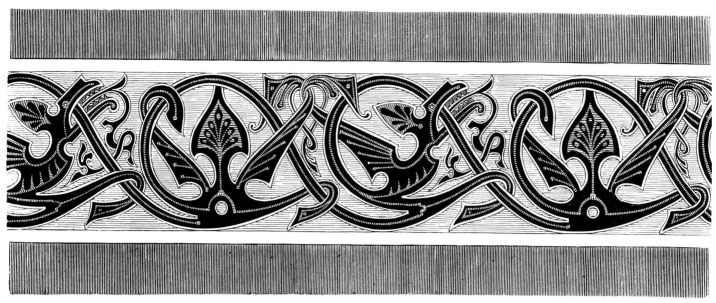

Norwegian border design. *Gewerbehalle, Vol. 10*

Spanish fabric designs, 15th century. *Pattern Design*

Hungarian marquetry from St. Catherine's Church in Kremnitz. *Workshop, Vol. 15*

Miscellaneous Designs continued

Medieval Russian manuscript ornament. *Outlines*

Norwegian architectural ornament, 13th century. *Gewerbehalle, Vol. 10*

Miscellaneous Designs continued

Slavic folk designs, 13th century. *L'Art, Vol. 35*

Czech painted ceiling. *Gewerbehalle, Vol. 6*

Miscellaneous Designs continued

Spanish silk, 14th century. *L'Art, Vol. 12*

Spanish ceramic tile, 16th century. *L'Art, Vol. 27*

Hungarian silk pattern, 15th century. *Workshop, Vol. 8*

Czech border design, 18th century. *Gewerbehalle, Vol. 8*

SOURCES

ART JOURNAL. New York: James S. Virtue, 1854-1861.

ENCYCLOPEDIA OF ORNAMENT. Shaw, Henry. Edinburgh: 1842.

ENGLISH ENCYCLOPEDIA: *A Collection of Treatises Illustrative of the Arts and Sciences* (10 vols.). London: G. Kearsley of Fleet Street, 1802.

GEWERBEHALLE: *Organ fur den Fortschritt in allen Zweigen der Kunst-Industrie.* Schnorr, Julius, ed. Vienna: 1862-1883.

INDUSTRY OF NATIONS; full title, *The Industry of All Nations,* (a special issue of the *Art Journal* devoted to the Crystal Palace Exhibition). London: George Virtue, 1851.

L'ART; full title, *L'Art Pour Tous, Encyclopedie de l'Art Industriel et Decoratif.* Reiber, Emile, ed. Paris: A. Morel et C., 1861-1906.

OUTLINES; full title, *Outlines of Ornament in the Leading Styles.* Audsley, W. & G. New York: Scribner, 1882.

PATTERN DESIGN; original title, *Traditional Methods of Pattern Designing.* Christie, Archibald H. New York: Dover Publications, 1967 (original publication date, 1910).

PERIOD FURNISHINGS: *An Encyclopedia of Ornament.* Clifford, C.R. New York: Clifford & Lawton, 1914.

STUDIO: *An Illustrated Magazine of Fine and Applied Art.* London: 1880-1902.

TYPE & DESIGN; full title, *Art Nouveau & Early Art Deco Type & Design.* Menten, Theodore. New York: Dover Publications, 1972.

VICTORIAN STENCILS; full title, *Victorian Stencils for Design and Decoration.* Gillon, Edmund V. New York: Dover Publications, 1968.

WEAPONS & ARMOR. Sietsema, Robert. New York: Hart Publishing Company, 1978.

WORKSHOP, THE: *A Monthly Journal, devoted to Progress of the Useful Arts,* (English language edition of *Gewerbehalle*). Baumer, W., and J. Schnorr, eds. New York: E. Steiger, 1868-1883.

HART PICTURE ARCHIVES

AMERICAN DESIGNS

THE ANIMAL KINGDOM

BORDERS & FRAMES

CHAIRS

COMPENDIUM

DESIGNS OF THE ANCIENT WORLD

DINING & DRINKING

EUROPEAN DESIGNS

GOODS & MERCHANDISE

HOLIDAYS

HUMOR, WIT, & FANTASY

JEWELRY

ORIENTAL DESIGNS

TRADES & PROFESSIONS

WEAPONS & ARMOR

WEATHER

TITLES IN PREPARATION

FACES

JARS, BOWLS, & VASES

TYPOGRAPHICAL ORNAMENTS